EXPLORING THE SUBATOMIC WORLD

Understanding
HIGGS
BOSONS

Fred Bortz

Cavendish
Square

New York

To Rosie, whose field helps people gain a mass of knowledge

Published in 2016 by Cavendish Square Publishing, LLC
243 5th Avenue, Suite 136, New York, NY 10016

Copyright © 2016 by Cavendish Square Publishing, LLC

First Edition

Cataloging-in-Publication Data

Bortz, Fred.
Understanding Higgs bosons / by Fred Bortz.
p. cm. — (Exploring the subatomic world)
Includes index.
ISBN 978-1-50260-550-4 (hardcover) ISBN 978-1-50260-551-1 (ebook)
1. Higgs bosons. 2. Particles (Nuclear physics) — Juvenile literature.
I. Bortz, Fred, 1944-. II. Title.
QC793.5.B62 B67 2016
539.7'21—d23

Editorial Director: David McNamara
Editor: Andrew Coddington
Copy Editor: Cynthia Roby
Art Director: Jeff Talbot
Designer: Stephanie Flecha
Senior Production Manager: Jennifer Ryder-Talbot
Production Editor: Renni Johnson
Photo Research: J8 Media

The photographs in this book are used by permission and through the courtesy of: Crady von Pawlak/Getty Images, cover; Sakkmesterke/Shutterstock.com, throughout; Fabrice Coffrini/AFP/GettyImages, 5; Public domain/File:Democritus in Thomas Stanley History of Philosophy.jpg/Wikimedia Commons, 9; Public domain/Thomas Phillips/File:John Dalton by Thomas Phillips, 1835.jpg/Wikimedia Commons, 10; Public domain/File:DIMendeleevCab.jpg/Wikimedia Commons, 11; Source: File:Rutherford gold foil experiment results.svg/Wikimedia Commons, 13; Cambridge University Library, courtesy AIP Emilio Segre Visual Archives, Rutherford Collection, 16; SSPL/Getty Images, 20; Thomas Forget, 21; Imagno/Getty Images, 24; SSPL/Getty Images, 25; Hulton Archive/Getty Images, 27; Thomas Forget, 28; AIP Emilio Segre Visual Archives, Yukawa Collection, 31; Public domain/Nobel Foundation/File:Dirac 4.jpg/Wikimedia Commons, 33; AIP Emilio Segre Visual Archives, 36; Science Museum of London/Science and Society Picture Library/File:60-inch cyclotron, c 1930s. This shows the (9660569583).jpg/Wikimedia Commons, 38; Courtesy Brookhaven National Laboratory, 41, Photo, Inc./Science Source/Getty Images, 43; Courtesy Brookhaven National Laboratory, 44; Source: Andres Rojas/File:The Standard Model.svg/Wikimedia Commons, 48; ATLAS and CMS © CERN, 49; © 2005 CERN, 50; Public domain/Energy.gov/File:HD.3F.001 (11086394836).jpg/Wikimedia Commons, 51; © CERN, 53.

Printed in the United States of America

Contents

Introduction

What is matter? That is one of humanity's most ancient questions about nature. Yet it continues to be at the heart of some of the most exciting modern research. To study the tiniest particles of matter, scientists have designed and built some of the largest, most powerful, and most complex machines in the world. Their discoveries have changed our fundamental understanding of matter, and each discovery has led to even more questions. That is certainly true of the story of a long-sought subatomic particle called the **Higgs boson**.

When physicists—scientists who study the physical world of matter and energy—officially announced the Higgs boson discovery by the Large Hadron Collider (LHC) at the European Organization for Nuclear Research (CERN) in Switzerland on July 4, 2012, it made headlines around the world. Yet some still questioned whether the discovery met all the criteria for the elusive particle.

Further research persuaded most doubters that the particle was indeed the Higgs. In 2013, the Nobel Prize committee honored Peter Higgs (1929–) and François Englert (1932–)

Men of the Hour. Peter Higgs (*right*) and François Englert respond to a cheering audience at CERN on July 4, 2012, where two teams of scientists announced the discovery of the Higgs boson after a nearly fifty-year quest.

What are CERN, ATLAS, and CMS?

The announcement of the 2013 Nobel Prize in Physics included three acronyms: CERN, ATLAS, and CMS. CERN stands for the original French name of the institution where researchers discovered the Higgs boson, Conseil Européen pour la Recherche Nucléaire (European Council for Nuclear Research). That acronym is still used even though "Conseil" in the name has been replaced by "Organisation."

ATLAS and CMS are two of the detectors that scientists use at the LHC. ATLAS stands for A Toroidal LHC Apparatus, referring to its doughnut (torus) shape and reflecting the fact that physicists love to invent acronyms. CMS stands for Compact Muon Solenoid. A solenoid is a coil of wire that acts as an electromagnet. A muon, as you will read later, is a type of subatomic particle that may reveal where a Higgs boson was produced.

with that year's award in physics "for the theoretical discovery of a mechanism that contributes to our understanding of the origin of mass of subatomic particles, and which recently was confirmed through the discovery of the predicted fundamental particle, by the ATLAS and CMS experiments at CERN's Large Hadron Collider."

Rarely is a Nobel Prize awarded so soon after a discovery, but this one was fifty years in the making. Higgs and two groups of physicists, including Englert and four others, had proposed their theories in 1964. Many scientists were wondering whether they would live long enough to see their ideas validated or ruled out by experimental evidence. Indeed, Englert's collaborator Robert Brout (born 1928) died in 2011 while the LHC was still gathering the key data that led to the award. Many physicists think he would have shared the Nobel Prize, which is only given to living scientists and never divided more than three ways. Others, including Higgs, argue that Tom Kibble (1932–), lead author of a paper on the subject with Gerald Guralnik (1936–2014) and Carl Richard Hagen (1937–), deserved a share of the prize.

The discovery of the Higgs boson was historic because it completed the set of particles that physicists expected in what they call the Standard Model of particle physics. But that discovery is not the end of the story of the quest to understand the subatomic world. As is often the case in science, many unanswered questions remain. They are like dangling threads of a carefully woven fabric, and no one can be sure what might unravel when other scientists give those loose ends a tug. Just as science is built around questions such as this, so is this book. Read on to learn about the Higgs boson, why it is important, and what remains to be discovered.

1 INSIDE
THE ATOM

This book is the story of a great question of ancient times and what it means for modern science. Twenty-five centuries ago, the Greek philosopher Leucippus and his student Democritus wondered, "What is the nature of matter?"

Leucippus and Democritus imagined cutting a piece of matter into smaller and smaller pieces until it could no longer be cut. They called the smallest piece of matter *atomos*, Greek for indivisible, from which our modern word **"atom"** derives. They decided that the properties of a substance depended on the shape and texture of its atoms. Water atoms were round and smooth, while atoms of rocks were hard and sharp.

As Democritus neared the end of his life, Greek philosophy entered a "golden era" in which Socrates, Aristotle, Plato, and other great thinkers used the power of logic to discover the "truth" about the natural world.

When Aristotle described the fundamental makeup of matter, he spoke not of atoms but of four elements that, in differing combinations, comprised everything in the world: earth, air, fire, and water.

Fundamental Particles

Neither ancient school of thought was exactly correct. Aristotle was right about a relatively small number of natural elements that make up the world, but water is not one of them. Leucippus

Atomic Visionary. The ancient Greek philosopher Democritus was the leader of a school of thought that described matter as being made of tiny pieces that cannot be divided further. Our modern word "atom" comes from the Greek word *atomos,* meaning indivisible.

and Democritus were on the right track about fundamental bits that comprise substances, but they were very wrong about the details. For example, water is not an element made of atoms. It is a **compound**, and its basic units are **molecules** formed from two hydrogen atoms combined with one oxygen atom (H_2O). We now know of approximately ninety natural elements, plus nearly thirty human-made ones.

The modern idea of atoms, molecules, elements, and compounds can be traced to English meteorologist John Dalton (1766–1844). In the early years of the nineteenth century, Dalton began studying the gases of the air. He soon realized that by adding the idea of molecules to the

John Dalton in 1835. Dalton drew on the ancient idea of tiny indivisible particles in his landmark 1810 book, *A New System of Chemical Philosophy*. The book stated that Democritus's atoms were actually molecules of chemical compounds, and that those molecules comprised indivisible atoms of chemical elements.

centuries-old concept of atoms, he could explain not only the way gases behaved, but also chemical reactions. In an 1810 book titled *A New System of Chemical Philosophy*, Dalton noted that the smallest unit of most substances was not an indivisible atom but a divisible molecule.

The idea of indivisible, fundamental particles is productive even today. But, as you will discover in later chapters, atoms and molecules are only the beginning of the story. Besides writing his famous book, Dalton determined the **atomic weight** of many elements. He set the atomic weight of hydrogen, the lightest element, to one unit, and based the atomic weight of other atoms on that. For example, water is a compound of one part hydrogen and eight parts oxygen by weight. Dalton assumed that a water molecule had one atom of each element and therefore set the atomic weight of oxygen at eight units. Later research showed that water molecules had two atoms of hydrogen and one of oxygen, so scientists corrected that result, setting the atomic weight of oxygen to sixteen.

Mendeleyev's Periodic Table

Using Dalton's approach, chemists identified more compounds and the elements that composed them, and they gradually developed a list of elements and their atomic weights. No one had detected individual atoms, but Dalton had given chemistry a new basic vocabulary based on elements and compounds, and atoms and molecules. But a major question remained: What makes one atom different from another? The first hint came from the work of Russian chemist Dmitry Ivanovich Mendeleyev (1834–1907), a professor at St. Petersburg University.

By the end of the 1860s, scientists knew of sixty-three elements and could see hints of similarities and patterns among their properties. They knew their atomic weights, their melting or boiling points, their densities (how much each cubic centimeter weighs), the way they combined with other elements, and the properties of the compounds they formed. Still, no one had come up with a successful classification scheme.

Early in 1869, Mendeleyev made a breakthrough. He arranged the elements in a chart with rows and columns. The first column was hydrogen alone. Helium was not yet known, so the next column began with lithium (atomic weight 7). Below that, he listed other elements from top to bottom in order of increasing atomic weight. When he reached sodium, which had similar chemical reactions to lithium, he started a new column. Repeating the process, he eventually had an array that not only had a place for

Mendeleyev in 1897. As scientists discovered more chemical elements, they began looking for an arrangement to classify them. In 1869, Dmitry Mendeleyev developed the periodic table of the elements, a system that placed elements in rows and columns. The modern version of that table can be found on the walls of physics classrooms and laboratories around the world.

all known elements but also had gaps where he predicted new elements would be found. He even predicted their atomic weights and densities.

Later discoveries of new elements proved Mendeleyev right, and his chart, which came to be called the **periodic table of the elements** because of its repeating structure, was established as one of the great ideas of chemistry. Modern periodic tables reverse the role of Mendeleyev's rows and columns, but the relationships he discovered are still valid.

What Makes One Atom Different from Another?

The periodic table helped scientists to organize the elements, but it left many important questions unanswered. As the number of known elements grew, scientists began questioning the idea that atoms were fundamental. They wondered if atoms were more like compounds than elements, built up from a small set of fundamental subatomic particles that combined in particular ways.

The first firm evidence of particles smaller than atoms came from J. J. Thomson (1856–1940) at the Cavendish Laboratory of Cambridge University in England. In 1897, Thomson described the discovery of a tiny bit of matter that we now call the electron. It was less than a thousandth as heavy as the lightest known atom, hydrogen, yet it had as much negative electrical charge as that atom might carry in positive charge. By then, scientists knew that electricity was related to chemical reactions, and thus it was probably important in atoms. Thomson's discovery suggested that atoms are held together by electric forces and composed of tiny negatively charged electrons and much heavier positively charged particles.

The discovery of the electron led scientists to think differently about the elements of the periodic table. Not only did the atoms increase in weight along the table's rows and columns, but they also increased in number of electrons, each atom having one more than its predecessor. Each element could now be labeled by a distinct **atomic number**—its number of electrons—as well as by its weight. Thomson began to think about the inner details of atoms, especially the large ones with lots of electrons. Since electrons were so light compared with the much greater mass of the atoms, he proposed that an atom was like a plum pudding with tiny electron plums scattered throughout an electrically positive mass. Other physicists imagined atoms differently, perhaps as tight clusters of positive and negative charges.

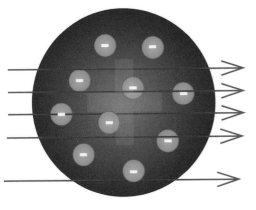

Many ideas seemed sensible, but which best represented nature? New Zealand–born Ernest Rutherford (1871–1937), a professor at the University of Manchester in England, had an idea about how to explore that question. Rutherford was world famous for earlier discoveries about **radioactivity**, including

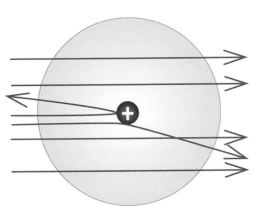

Rutherford's surprise. Ernest Rutherford realized that he could determine the inner structure of atoms by bombarding a thin metal foil with alpha particles. If atoms were like the "plum pudding" model (*top*), he expected very little, if any, scattering. He was surprised when a small fraction of the alpha particles bounced almost directly backwards. That result led him to conclude that most of an atom's mass is concentrated in a very tiny nucleus (*bottom*).

that it came in three forms, which he named **alpha, beta,** and **gamma rays.**

Rutherford's idea was to use beams of alpha rays (which he realized were particles) to study the structure of large atoms, such as gold. His technique was to send the alphas toward thin strips of metal foil and measure the **scattering,** or the pattern of the deflections produced by their interactions with the atoms in the foil. From that pattern, he expected to deduce the size, spacing, and perhaps even the shape or internal structure of those atoms. The first task, which he assigned to his student Hans Geiger (1882–1945), was to build an instrument that detected and counted alphas. They began their scattering experiments in 1909 and quickly noted that nearly all the alphas passed straight through the foil or deflected only slightly.

That was exactly what they would expect from Thomson's plum pudding atoms, except for one remaining puzzle: a few **alpha particles** were unaccounted for. Had those particles scattered beyond the detectors? If so, what was deflecting that small number of alphas so much, while almost all the rest passed nearly straight through the foil? Intrigued, but not wanting to divert Geiger from his detailed measurements, Rutherford decided that the task of looking for large-angle scattering would be good practice for Ernest Marsden (1889–1970), a young student just learning the techniques of research. Marsden found the missing alpha particles. Some went to the left or right of the original detectors, and astonishingly, a few even scattered backward.

By 1911, Rutherford was ready to announce his explanation to the world. He described atoms as miniature solar systems held together by electrical forces instead of gravity. Most of an atom is empty space. Tiny electrons,

Rutherford and the ABCs of Radioactivity

As a student in Thomson's laboratory between 1895 and 1898, Rutherford was among the first to study a phenomenon called radioactivity, first noted by Henri Becquerel (1852–1908) in 1896. Becquerel found that uranium was emitting some kind of energy that would darken photographic plates just as recently discovered X-rays did. Other scientists soon discovered other naturally occurring radioactive elements.

In 1898, Rutherford moved to McGill University in Montreal, Canada, where he stayed for ten years and made many major discoveries about radioactivity and radioactive elements. For example, by allowing radioactivity from various sources to strike different materials, Rutherford found that it took two different forms. The first, which he called alpha rays after the first letter of the Greek alphabet, carried a positive electric charge and could be stopped by a sheet of paper. The second form, beta rays, were negatively charged and much more penetrating.

In 1900, Becquerel determined that beta rays are electrons. That same year, Paul Villard (1860–1934) discovered even more penetrating radioactivity from radium. In 1903, Rutherford identified that as a separate type of radioactivity and called it gamma radiation. In 1907, he determined that alpha rays were helium nuclei (although this was before his discovery that an atom has a nucleus, so he did not use that term).

In 1908, he returned to England as a professor at Manchester University. It was there that he discovered the atomic nucleus in 1911. In 1914, he finally completed the Greek ABCs of radioactivity by showing that gamma rays were electromagnetic waves similar to X-rays but with even more energy.

like planets, have only a small fraction of the system's total mass and orbit a much more massive central body called the **nucleus** (plural: nuclei). The nucleus is very compact. Its large mass and positive charge are concentrated in about one ten-thousandth of the diameter of the atom. The emptiness of the atom explains why most alpha particles pass through it with little scattering. But on those rare occasions when a fast-moving alpha particle makes a nearly direct hit on a heavy nucleus, the alpha scatters sideways or even backward.

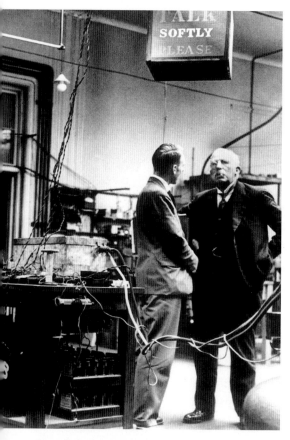

Ernest Rutherford in 1932. Rutherford (*right*) was an imposing man, known for his leadership and his powerful voice, which he sometimes had to tone down, as in this laboratory where the equipment used a microphone and sensitive amplifier.

Protons and Neutrons

Is the nucleus a fundamental particle? Rutherford and other scientists thought not. Nature seemed to have a basic unit of electric charge, and so most scientists thought that the nucleus would probably contain as many positive particles, which they called protons, as the atom had electrons.

But looking at the periodic table, they immediately realized things were not quite so simple. The atomic weight—or **atomic mass**, a term physicists prefer—of hydrogen is 1. Its atomic number is also 1. However, helium, with atomic number 2, has an atomic mass of four hydrogen atoms (or four atomic mass units). Farther up the periodic table, the problem is worse. Lead, for example, has atomic number 82 and atomic mass 207. Protons did not account for even half the mass of most nuclei.

As Rutherford reflected on the situation, he realized that the extra mass might have something to do with another question. Bodies with the same kind of electric charge repel each other, and the force between them becomes much more powerful as they get closer together. Containing so

Isotopes and Atomic Mass Units

In the periodic table, every atomic number is a whole number that is equal to the number of protons in that nucleus. The atomic masses are not whole numbers. There are two reasons for that. First, neutrons are slightly heavier than protons. Second, one nucleus of an element can have a different number of neutrons than another. For example, on Earth, approximately one hydrogen atom in 6,400 has a nucleus made up of one proton and one neutron. It is called deuterium and its atomic mass is slightly more than two protons.

Scientists use the term isotope to describe the different atomic weights that an element can have. The atomic mass listed in most periodic tables is the average mass of all the naturally occurring atoms of that element. To provide a standard atomic mass unit (AMU), scientists have agreed to set the mass of the most common isotope of carbon, with six protons and six neutrons, to exactly twelve AMU.

many positively charged protons packed close together, the nucleus would blow itself to bits, or so it seemed. Whatever is giving the nucleus extra mass must also be responsible for holding the nucleus together. Rutherford theorized that the rest of the mass came from electrically neutral particles with masses about the same as protons. He called them neutrons, and he turned out to be right (although they were not detected until 1932).

The discovery of the neutron established the basic atomic structure we now know: a tiny but massive nucleus of positively charged protons and electrically neutral neutrons, occupying only about a ten-thousandth of the atom's diameter, surrounded by light electrons in equal number to the protons. Still, many questions remained about atoms and subatomic particles, including the nature of radioactivity and the powerful nuclear force that binds the nucleus together.

Once again, scientists had reason to believe they had found the fundamental particles of all matter. Everything was made of atoms, and atoms consisted of protons, neutrons, and electrons. But they were wrong in three significant ways.

First, to explain beta radiation, physicists had to propose tiny particles called neutrinos. Neutrinos are not found inside nuclei, yet they can be produced inside them. Second, surprising discoveries revealed many types of matter—a whole "zoo" of particles—that are not part of atoms. And third, protons, neutrons, and some other particles in that zoo are not actually fundamental particles. They are made of even smaller particles called **quarks**.

Lurking behind those discoveries was the Higgs boson. But no one yet knew enough about the subatomic world to imagine that it might exist!

2 DISCOVERING
the Particle "Zoo"

Rutherford's discovery of the atomic nucleus was one of several revolutionary developments in physics during the early years of the twentieth century. Perhaps the two most famous are the **theory of relativity** and **quantum mechanics**, which together transformed the way science views space and time, matter and energy, waves and particles. Both of those were important to developing a full understanding of atoms and radioactivity.

Rutherford recognized that his planetary model of the atom was not perfect. The biggest problem was with the well-established equations of **electromagnetism**. Those equations showed that an electric charge moving in a curved path would radiate electromagnetic waves—a form of energy that includes light—and it would gradually lose energy. That meant that orbiting electrons would soon spiral into the nucleus, and that would be the end of the atom.

So either the model of orbiting electrons was wrong, or the laws of electromagnetism were different for atoms. Which was it?

Seeing the Light

At least two clues to the answer had already emerged. Both lay in phenomena dealing with light. Clue number one came in 1900, when German physicist Max Planck (1858–1947) invented what he thought was merely a mathematical trick to explain the **spectrum**, or intensity of different colors, in the glow from a hot body. Instead of allowing light energy to come in any amount, like liquid, his formula was based on having tiny energy packets, called "quanta" (singular: **quantum**), like grains of sand.

When he compared his formula to measured results, it fit surprisingly well. Planck had put an adjustable value into his formula, expecting that it might be different for different temperatures. But to his astonishment, the same value worked for every temperature. Nature was sending a signal that this value—known today as Planck's constant—was

Quantum Pioneer Max Planck. In order to explain the shape of the spectrum of a glowing hot body, Planck introduced the quantum, which he considered a mathematical trick. It turned out to be real.

important, but he couldn't figure out why. In fact, even though his formula worked, he could not accept that light was grainy. How could it be, since a classic experiment by Thomas Young (1773–1829) in 1801—ninety-nine years earlier—proved that light was a wave phenomenon?

The mystery deepened in 1905 when Albert Einstein (1879–1955) investigated other experiments and concluded that Planck's light quanta (which later came to be known as photons) were real. The evidence was in a phenomenon called the **photoelectric effect**, in which light can knock electrons free from a piece of metal. The brightness of the light doesn't matter, only its color (or frequency of the electromagnetic wave).

Each metal had a different threshold frequency. Below the threshold, the most intense light failed to eject electrons. Above it, the dimmest light could cause an electric current. Einstein knew that the energy of Planck's quanta became greater as the frequency increased. He also knew that it would take a certain amount of energy to eject electrons from a metal. Thus he proposed that the threshold frequency for ejection corresponded to the energy of one light quantum. Experiments on photoelectricity supported the conclusion.

Clue number two was in the line spectrum of electrically excited gases in a tube (such as the familiar red glow of neon lights). A line spectrum is different from the continuous spectrum that led Planck to the quantum. A continuous spectrum is the color of the glow from hot bodies. When the

Line Spectrum of Hydrogen. When the atoms of an element or compound are excited by electricity or a flame, they produce a characteristic line spectrum, like this one of hydrogen.

Light: Waves or Particles?

What is light? That simple question has driven human curiosity throughout history. Among the first to pursue that question were two seventeenth-century scientists who are considered to be among the most important of their time, or of any time: Sir Isaac Newton (1642–1727) and Christiaan Huygens (1629–1695).

But what is light made of? Newton and Huygens disagreed, each giving a detailed explanation of reflection, refraction, and all other observed phenomena of light. Newton decided that light must be made of tiny particles, which he called corpuscles. Huygens was more comfortable with the idea that light was a wave. Both

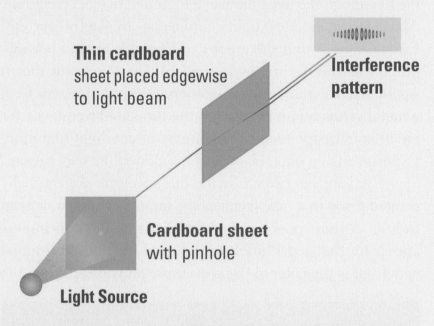

Thin cardboard sheet placed edgewise to light beam

Interference pattern

Cardboard sheet with pinhole

Light Source

Young's Experiment. When Thomas Young performed this experiment in 1801, it seemed to settle the question of whether light was a wave or a stream of particles. The interference pattern convinced everyone that light was a wave.

men had died long before Thomas Young (1773–1829) performed an experiment in 1801 to settle the wave-particle question.

Young created a narrow sunbeam by passing sunlight through a pinhole. He then split the beam in two with a piece of thin cardboard placed edgewise. Instead of casting a sharp, thin shadow, as would be expected if the card had divided a stream of particles, the split beam produced a series of light and dark bands—an effect called interference—which occurs when waves meet. Young's experiment proved once and for all that light was a wave phenomenon—or so scientists thought at the time. Planck was certainly persuaded. That's why he viewed the quantum as a mathematical trick even though it explained the spectrum of a glowing hot object where a wave explanation failed.

light from that glow passes through a glass prism or another instrument that spreads out its colors, it produces a band of hues like a rainbow. The spectrum of an electrically excited gas is not a band but a series of distinct lines. It contains only certain frequencies and no others.

Several scientists had discovered mathematical patterns in the frequencies of the lines in the hydrogen spectrum, but they didn't have an explanation for them. In 1913, Danish physicist Niels Bohr (1885–1962) put the clues together and modified Rutherford's planetary model of the atom. Bohr proposed that electrons have certain natural orbits, each with its own energy level, in which they would not radiate. Why those natural levels and not others? Bohr looked at Planck's constant and saw that it had the same units as a mechanical quantity known as angular momentum. What if the angular momentum of allowed orbits was a whole number times Planck's constant?

Bohr did the mathematics. He calculated the energy difference between various electron energy levels. He assumed that when an electron drops from one orbit to another with lower energy, the energy difference appears as a quantum of light. That produced a calculated line spectrum for hydrogen, and the calculations matched what people had observed. The importance of Bohr's energy levels and Planck's constant were changing what people understood about the subatomic world.

That was the beginning of a new field of physics called quantum mechanics. Over the next two decades, many great physicists developed a large body of new mathematics to describe the behavior of matter and energy at the atomic level. One result solved the problem of orbiting electrons in Rutherford's description of the atom. If light, long understood as a wave phenomenon, could sometimes behave like a stream of particles, could particles like electrons sometimes behave like waves?

In 1924, Louis-Victor de Broglie (1892–1987) explored that question in his doctoral dissertation. He devised a formula that used Planck's constant to relate an electron's wavelength to its speed, and discovered that the circumference of the allowed orbits in Bohr's theory was a whole number of

Neils Bohr in 1930. Bohr developed a theory that electrons in atoms only had certain allowed orbits and emitted a quantum of light when dropping from a higher level to a lower one. That successfully explained the mathematical patterns that had been observed in the frequencies of spectral lines for hydrogen.

Electrons As Wave Functions

Schrödinger's wave functions are puzzling to people who are used to thinking of particles as having a definite position and motion. To understand what a wave function means, imagine an object

bouncing back and forth so fast on a very tight spring that all you can see is a blur. Near the ends of its bounces, the object moves more slowly and its appearance is less blurry. So where is the object? It could be anywhere along the path, but it is more likely to be near one of the less blurry ends than in the middle. In quantum mechanics, the blur is the object.

Erwin Schrödinger. Schrödinger developed a basic equation of quantum mechanics that described particles as wave functions. In 1956, the Austrian Academy of Sciences presented him with an award for lifetime achievement and established the Erwin Schrödinger Prize for excellence and achievements in science or mathematics in his honor.

electron wavelengths. Now instead of being particles orbiting the nucleus, electrons could be considered as waves wrapped around the nucleus. Erwin Schrödinger (1887–1961) used de Broglie's idea to develop an equation that described particles by their "wave functions."

Quantum mechanics also led to a set of four "**quantum numbers**" that described the "state" of an electron in an atom. The mathematics also led Wolfgang Pauli (1900–1958) to an important idea about electrons in atoms, which is now called the Pauli exclusion principle. That principle states that no two electrons in an atom can have the same set of quantum numbers. Moving to higher atomic numbers on the list of elements, the four quantum numbers follow a pattern that matches the periodic properties of elements in Mendeleyev's table. After more than sixty years of wondering, quantum mechanics provided science with an explanation for what made that table periodic.

Relativity and Radioactivity

The year 1905 is often called Albert Einstein's "miracle year" because he published three scientific articles that each transformed physicists' understanding of the world. As noted, his article explaining the photoelectric effect elevated Planck's quantum from a mathematical trick to an actual physical phenomenon. That article set physicists on the path to quantum mechanics.

In another article, the phenomenon of **Brownian motion**, in which pollen grains suspended in a liquid followed a jiggling, jerky path, was explored. Einstein used a mathematical description of heat, called statistical mechanics, to analyze that motion. He noted that the movement of the pollen grains matched exactly what would be expected if molecules of the liquid collided with them. Until that analysis, atoms and molecules were as theoretical as Planck's quanta. Thanks to Einstein, people recognized Brownian motion as experimental evidence of their existence.

The third article is the best known to non-scientists. It described what is known as the Special Theory of Relativity. That theory led physicists to a new understanding of space, time, and the speed of light. It states that the measurement of an object's motion only has meaning when measured relative to other objects. It also states that the relative speed of two objects can never be faster than the speed of light. (The word

Albert Einstein in the Early 1930s. Einstein's theory of relativity remains one of the most well-known in science. Its most famous equation, $E = mc^2$, transformed mass and energy from separate quantities into two faces of the same thing.

"Special" refers to the fact that it deals with constant relative velocities between objects. The General Theory of Relativity, which Einstein developed over the next decade and published in 1916, describes accelerated or changing relative motion.)

The most famous equation from the Theory of Relativity is $E = mc^2$, which implies that mass is actually a form of energy. In words, it states that E, the energy of a bit of matter such as a subatomic particle, is equal to m, the mass of that particle, times the square of c, the speed of light. (The square of a quantity is that quantity multiplied by itself.)

That equation is important for understanding radioactivity. One of the most important principles in physics is the law of conservation of energy. That law states that in any physical interaction or process, energy can change from one form to another, but the total amount of energy can never change. The discovery of radioactivity posed this question: Since energy must be conserved, from where does the energy of alpha, beta, and gamma rays come?

When studying alpha radiation, physicists noted that all the alpha particles from the radioactive decay of a particular nucleus have the same kinetic energy (energy of motion). From where does that kinetic energy come? The answer is in the equation $E = mc^2$. When a "parent" nucleus undergoes alpha decay, the result is a new "daughter" nucleus, which is smaller than the parent in both atomic number and atomic mass. The daughter, with two fewer protons and two fewer neutrons, has an atomic number two less than the parent, and its mass is less by approximately four atomic mass units.

Based on your everyday experience, you might think the difference in mass between parent and daughter should be exactly equal to the mass of the alpha particle—but that is not so. Part of the mass of a nucleus comes from the "binding energy" that holds its protons and neutrons together. Binding energy has a negative value since energy has to be added to break a nucleus apart. Of all the nuclei, the alpha particle is the most tightly bound. Therefore, when inside the parent nucleus, its mass is less than that of two protons plus two neutrons.

When a radioactive nucleus emits an alpha particle, some mass is lost. That lost mass shows up as kinetic energy of that alpha particle. Careful measurements of the masses of parent and daughter nuclei have shown kinetic energy to be equal to that lost mass times c^2, exactly enough to satisfy the law of conservation of energy.

Energy is also conserved in gamma

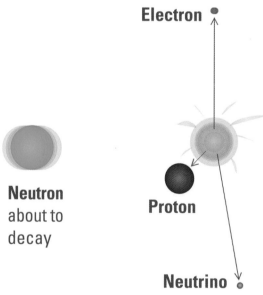

Electron

Neutron
about to
decay

Proton

Neutrino

Beta Radiation. When studying what happens when a radioactive nucleus produces a beta ray (which is an electron), physicists realized that a very small, undetected electrically neutral particle must also be emitted. They named it the neutrino.

radiation, though it is harder to measure. Gamma radiation never occurs alone. It always follows an alpha or beta ray. In those cases, the daughter nucleus is in an "excited" state and then quickly drops to a state of lower energy by emitting a gamma ray photon. That process is similar to the way the electrons in an atom drop from a higher energy level to a lower one, emitting the photons of visible light in their line spectra.

However, in studying radioactivity that produces beta rays, physicists had a problem. Unlike alpha radiation, the emitted **beta particles** do not all have the same energy. Instead, their energies can be anywhere in the range from zero to a maximum value. That maximum value was what would be expected from the lost mass. However, in most cases the beta carries off less than the maximum, leaving some energy unaccounted for.

Pauli was the first to suggest an explanation in 1930, which was further developed by Italian-born Enrico Fermi (1901–1954) in 1933 and 1934, after the neutron had been detected. Pauli proposed that to account for the missing energy, another particle was also emitted in addition to the electron. Fermi proposed that in beta radiation, a neutron in a nucleus becomes a proton and emits an electron (the beta particle). Other conservation laws also would have to apply. In any interaction, the total momentum (mass times velocity) of all the particles has to be the same before and after the event. Since the momentum before the emission was zero, the mystery particle must have the same momentum as the electron but in the opposite direction. Knowing the momentum and energy enabled physicists to calculate that particle's mass, and the result showed that it had to be very small, perhaps even zero.

Another conservation law says that the total electric charge must not change. Before the decay, the neutron has zero charge.

After the decay, the proton and electron have equal and opposite charges, adding to zero. That means the other particle would have be electrically neutral. With no charge and very little mass, it would be very hard to detect directly. So Fermi gave it the Italian name neutrino, which means "little neutral one." As physicists learned more about beta decay, the neutrino became widely accepted, although it was not detected until 1956.

Non-Atomic Matter

People love science jokes. One that has been popular for some time is: "You can't trust atoms. They make up everything."

Physicists appreciate wordplay, so they laugh as hard as anyone at the double meaning of "make up" in that one-liner. But they also know it is wrong. The neutrino is an example of a particle that is not found in atoms. Does that make it non-atomic matter? Most physicists would say no, because it can emerge from a nucleus undergoing beta decay. That means it is related to atomic matter as we know it.

Beginning in the mid-1930s, physicists realized that there is more to the subatomic world than protons, neutrons, electrons, and neutrinos. In trying to understand radioactivity, they realized that other fundamental forces exist besides gravity and electromagnetism. For example, electric forces are attractive between particles with opposite charges, like positive protons and negative electrons. But like charges repel each other. Electric attraction or repulsion becomes much stronger as the distance between the particles decreases.

That attraction or repulsion follows what is known as an inverse square law. If the distance between them is cut in half, the force is four (2×2) times as great. If it is reduced to one-third, it increases to nine (3×3) times as much. Since a nucleus is about one ten-thousandth as large as an atom, the repulsive force between two protons in the nucleus is about one hundred million times as large as the attraction between a proton and an electron in an atom. Clearly the nucleus needs a very powerful force to keep it from blowing apart.

Physicists call that force the **strong nuclear force** or simply the **strong interaction**. (A second nuclear force, called the **weak nuclear force** or **weak interaction**, is related to the process of beta decay, described above.) The strong

Hideki Yukawa. Yukawa developed a theory to explain the strong nuclear force based on the exchange of particles known as pions between protons and neutrons in a nucleus.

force has to be much stronger than the electromagnetic force at distances as small as the nucleus, but much weaker than electromagnetism at larger distances. But what is it? Quantum mechanics clearly had something to say about that, but the answer was not obvious.

Physicists had begun to develop theories that combined quantum mechanics with the laws of electromagnetism. In those theories, the electromagnetic force was the result of electrically charged particles exchanging photons, which have no mass and travel at the speed of light. Even though those theories were incomplete in 1935, Hideki Yukawa (1907–1981) of Japan found a way to adapt some of their ideas to explain the way the strong force worked. He developed a theory that the nucleus was held together by exchanging particles now known as "pions" with a mass about 250 times that of an electron.

Antimatter

Some readers of this book may have heard of antimatter. Like the neutrino, photon, and Higgs boson, antimatter was predicted to exist before it was found. And like Planck and the light quantum, the physicist whose mathematics predicted it did not think it was real.

In 1928, Paul A. M. Dirac (1902–1984) combined Schrödinger's equation with Einstein's Special Theory of Relativity and got a surprise. His equation had solutions that described not only negatively charged electrons, but also particles with the same mass but a positive charge. Other quantum mechanical properties of those particles were also reversed.

The equation made similar predictions for all other subatomic particles. None of those antiparticles or antimatter, as they were called, had ever been seen. So Dirac and most physicists thought they were accidents of mathematics. In 1929 and 1930, two physicists observed particles in cosmic rays that seemed to be positively charged electrons, but they did not follow up fully. Then in 1932, a journal article by Carl D. Anderson (who later discovered

At first glance, adding those pions within the nucleus would add mass or, equivalently, energy. That seemed to violate conservation of energy, but quantum mechanics provided a way to avoid a problem. Werner Heisenberg (1901–1976) noted that the mathematics of quantum mechanics led to what has been called the Uncertainty Principle. In physics, measurements always have a limit to their precision, which is sometimes called the uncertainty. Heisenberg's Uncertainty Principle states that the value of an energy measurement has a minimum uncertainty the muon) reported a firm discovery of Dirac's predicted antielectrons, calling them positrons.

When a particle and its antiparticle meet, they annihilate each other. Their mass turns into energy in the form of a pair of photons. For physicists, antimatter poses a puzzle. Dirac's equation shows no favoritism between matter and antimatter, so they would expect both forms to have been created in equal amounts at the beginning of the universe. Yet matter dominates in the present universe, so more of it must have been created in the beginning. No one has succeeded in explaining why that is so.

Antimatter Matters. Paul Dirac, shown here in his official Nobel Prize photograph, shared that award for physics with Erwin Schrödinger in 1933. He modified Schrödinger's wave equation to fit with relativity and unexpectedly predicted the existence of antimatter.

that is related to the time interval used to measure it. If you multiply the minimum uncertainty by the time interval, you get Planck's constant. So if the time interval is very short, the uncertainty in energy can be as large as the mass of a pion without violating the law of conservation of energy. The pion in that case can be considered a "virtual" pion, but it can become real by adding enough energy to a nucleus to release it.

Since nothing can travel faster than light, Yukawa's theory considered time intervals so short that the pion could never leave the nucleus. That led to his estimated value for its mass. So the pion, though not yet discovered, joined the neutrino on the list of subatomic particles. Of course, scientists began looking for pions right away. The most likely place to find them was in cosmic rays, which are very energetic particles that stream down from space to Earth.

In 1936, Carl D. Anderson (1905–1991) and Seth Neddermeyer (1907–1988), Anderson's first graduate student at the California Institute of Technology, discovered cosmic ray particles that had about the expected mass of Yukawa's pion. But they didn't have the other properties that Yukawa expected. Instead, they looked like electrons in every way except for their heavier mass. They were what we now call muons. The muon turned out to be the first of many new subatomic particles that physicists would discover over the middle part of the twentieth century. As their number grew, physicists began speaking of a "particle zoo."

Every member of that zoo was related to protons, neutrons, electrons, and neutrinos in certain ways, but some had strange properties that were difficult to explain. In many ways, the subatomic zoo resembled the list of chemical elements before the discovery of the periodic table. It would take a twentieth-century physicist named Murray Gell-Mann (1929–) to sort it all out. Building on Gell-Mann's work, physicists eventually developed what is now known as The Standard Model of particle physics.

The Standard Model also led to questions about the masses of the different subatomic beasts in the zoo. Answering those questions would eventually bring fame to Peter Higgs, François Englert, and their colleagues.

3 QUARKS,
Leptons, and Bosons

When Anderson and Neddermeyer discovered the muon, a famous physicist quipped, "Who ordered that?" He was referring to the fact that the muon was not part of an atom like its smaller sibling, the electron. It would take the discovery of many more unexpected subatomic particles and several decades of research before physicists finally understood how the muon and the rest of the particle zoo fit together. To tell the story of the zoo, we begin with cosmic rays.

Cosmic Rays

When scientists first began to study radioactivity, they noticed that it would produce ions by knocking electrons out of atoms. They were also aware that the air always has some level of ionization. So it was natural to think that the ionization of the air was caused by radioactive material below the ground.

Taking to the Sky for Science. This 1912 photo shows Victor Hess about to ascend in a hydrogen balloon so he can determine the source of ionizing radiation. Many scientists thought the radiation came from Earth's rocks, but Hess showed it was coming from outside the planet.

However, when scientists measured the ionization at different heights, including the top of the Eiffel Tower, they noticed that ionization increased as they got farther from the ground.

In 1912, Victor Hess (1883–1964) rode in a balloon several times to altitudes as high as 18,000 feet (5,486 meters) and found that the radiation was twice as much at maximum height than at the ground. This was true at all times of the day and night. From that, Hess concluded that radiation was reaching Earth from space. Other scientists confirmed his discovery and called the radiation cosmic rays. But what were those rays?

Physicists used a detector called the cloud chamber to answer this question. The chamber works by using a similar principle to the one that enables us to see where an airplane is flying by the tiny exhaust particles (resembling a form of vapor) trailing behind it. At that height, the atmosphere contains water vapor that is ready to condense into tiny droplets or ice crystals. The exhaust particles serve as condensation sites, and a long thin cloud forms along the plane's path.

A cloud chamber contains water or alcohol vapor near its condensation point. When radioactivity or a cosmic ray particle passes through, it produces a trail of ions that serve as condensation points. Scientists developed techniques to identify the particles from their trails. For example, they used magnetic fields that caused electrically charged particles to follow curved paths. That allowed them to see the paths of alpha particles, beta particles (electrons), and protons. The positively charged alphas and protons curved in one direction, while the negatively charged betas curved in the opposite direction.

In 1932, Carl Anderson noticed some trails that looked exactly like the paths of electrons but curved in the direction that showed they were positively charged. He had discovered positrons, the first known particles of antimatter. He and Neddermeyer found muons in 1936 in a similar way. They noticed trails of negatively charged particles that did not curve as sharply as electrons with the same energy. They used that to measure the mass, which was close to that predicted for Yukawa's pions, but the particles' other properties matched electrons exactly.

The discovery of those previously unknown subatomic particles in cosmic rays was the first glimpse into a subatomic world that no one had anticipated. Furthermore, studies of muons showed that they were unstable particles. Sometimes their tracks in cloud chambers would end abruptly, only to be replaced by the track of an electron. As in the case of beta decay, the electron didn't carry all the energy of the muon, including the energy due to its mass. Physicists suspected that the decay also produced a neutrino. In fact, they would eventually discover that the decay produced two different types of neutrino.

Particle Accelerators

By the early 1930s, to learn more about what held nuclei together, physicists began trying to break them apart. They built machines to create intense, controllable beams of particles that would smash into targets. By then, Rutherford had returned to Cambridge University to head the Cavendish Laboratory. There, under his leadership, John Cockcroft (1897–1967) and Ernest Walton (1903–1995) built one of the first particle accelerators. In 1932, they became the first to succeed in what many people called "splitting the atom."

They used high voltage to accelerate protons toward a lithium target. A lithium nucleus has three protons and four neutrons. When a proton with enough energy hits it just right, the result is four protons and four neutrons that organize themselves into two alpha particles.

Cockcroft and Walton's machine sped protons up along a straight line. It was the simplest example of what we now call a linear accelerator. To make more powerful beams, physicists envisioned several stages of acceleration. One way to do that is to have one linear accelerator following another. But to reach very high energies requires a very long machine.

An Early Cyclotron. Inventor of the cyclotron, Ernest O. Lawrence (*third from left*), stands surrounded by key scientists involved in the development of the 60-inch (152.4 cm) cyclotron, not long after its completion in 1939.

In 1931, Ernest Orlando Lawrence (1901–1958), a physics professor at the University of California at Berkeley, came up with a different design. His device, which he called a cyclotron, sent particles in circular paths, accelerating them faster with each pass. Lawrence's cyclotron design is based on a pancake-shaped vacuum chamber separated by a gap into two D-shaped regions or "dees." A magnetic field causes the particles to follow a semicircular path around that dee.

The particles to be accelerated enter the chamber near its center at one side of the gap. An alternating-current (AC) source creates high voltage across the gap, which accelerates the particles whenever they reach it. The rate of alternation matches the time it takes for the particles to go halfway around, so when they reach the gap again, the voltage further accelerates them. With each increase in speed, the particles move in a larger circle and finally leave the cyclotron at a very high speed near its outer edge and head toward their target.

How high is that speed? Suppose there are one thousand volts across the gap and the particles make five hundred complete circles, or one thousand gap crossings. Then the particles reach the energy that would be created by a one-million-volt battery. The only limits to the energy are the diameter of the chamber and the strength of the magnetic field. (A stronger field makes for tighter circles and thus more gap crossings before the particles reach the outer edge of the chamber.)

By the late 1930s, Lawrence was building machines so large that the particles reached a significant fraction of the speed of light. At that point, effects of the special theory of relativity required him to vary the frequency of the cyclotron's alternating current in order to produce further acceleration. He developed designs for new machines called synchrocyclotrons (or simply synchrotrons), but then World War II slowed his research. The delay turned out to be helpful. Building synchrotrons would have been difficult without new electronic technologies developed during the war.

Over the years since then, particle accelerators have become much larger and more powerful. (See *Understanding the Large Hadron Collider* in this series.) Although the first goal in building larger machines was to study nuclei, scientists soon realized that they could also produce artificial cosmic rays. That led to discoveries of new particles that would have been difficult or impossible to find in cosmic rays.

Cosmic ray studies did produce new subatomic discoveries through 1947. In that year, cosmic ray scientists found the first evidence of the pions predicted in Yukawa's theory of the strong force. They found both positively and negatively charged pions with about the expected mass, but not neutral ones, even though the theory predicted all three types. (Scientists in Lawrence's cyclotron laboratory found the neutral pion in 1949.) In addition, they found an unexpected set of positive, negative, and neutral particles about 970 times as heavy as electrons. They identified those unexpected particles with the symbol K and called them kaons.

The menu of particles now included several that no one had "ordered." And it was clear that those surprising discoveries were only the beginning. By the middle of the twentieth century, it was clear that more powerful particle accelerators would reveal many more surprises in the subatomic world.

Revealing the Subatomic Zoo

Thanks to advances in particle accelerators and detectors, the decades of the 1950s through the 1970s were filled with discoveries of new subatomic particles named after various

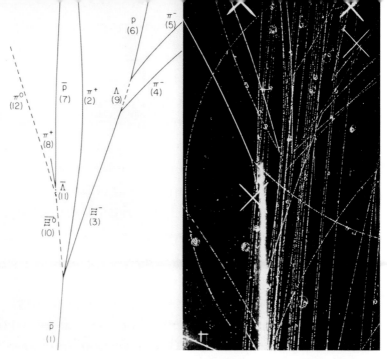

Bubble Chamber Tracks. From the 1950s to the 1970s, the development of more powerful particle accelerators and better detectors led to discoveries of numerous subatomic particles. On the right is a 1963 photograph from a bubble chamber detector, and on the left is an interpretation of its tracks produced by a collision between an antiproton entering at the bottom and a proton, resulting in a cascade of particles seen (*solid lines*) and unseen (*dotted lines*).

letters of the Greek or Latin alphabets. Those particles would often decay into other particles with less mass. By observing tracks that particles created in detectors, physicists were able to analyze not only those decays, but also the interactions that created new particles when accelerated particles such as protons or alpha particles hit a target.

They often described their results as conservation laws. These included conservation of energy (including the energy of mass according to $E = mc^2$), conservation of electric charge, and conservation of other quantum mechanical properties. In interactions governed by the strong nuclear force, one property was conserved for no obvious reason. They decided to call it strangeness. Protons, neutrons, and pions had strangeness of 0. Kaons and other particles called lambda, sigma, and delta had strangeness of 1. Their antiparticles had strangeness of –1.

Xi particles had a strangeness of 2, and their antiparticles had strangeness of −2.

As more elements were discovered, particle physicists found themselves in the same situation chemists were in a century earlier: the more particles they found, the more disorderly the subatomic world seemed to be. They began speaking of a particle zoo and the need for a modern-day Mendeleyev to organize it. That's when Murray Gell-Mann stepped up. In collaboration with Kazuhiko Nishijima (1926–2009), he described a pattern based on a mathematical idea called group theory. At the same time, Yuval Ne'eman (1925–2006) discovered the same pattern.

If that pattern was correct, there was an undiscovered particle with strangeness of 3 and a negative charge. Gell-Mann called it the omega minus after the last letter of the Greek alphabet. While experimental particle physicists searched for the omega minus, Gell-Mann and others, most notably George Zweig (1937–), were trying to find a physical basis for that mathematical pattern.

In 1964, both efforts yielded fruit. Scientists at Brookhaven National Laboratory in New York discovered the omega minus, and Gell-Mann published a paper proposing that protons, neutrons, and several other particles, which physicists called hadrons (from the Greek word meaning massive), are not fundamental particles. Rather, they are composed of smaller entities called quarks. (The word quark came from Gell-Mann's whimsical imagination. He pronounced it to rhyme with cork, but took its spelling from a phrase in a novel titled *Finnegan's Wake* by James Joyce.) Hadrons are subdivided into baryons (from the Greek word meaning heavy), which are composed of three quarks, and mesons, composed of two quarks. Baryons include protons and neutrons, while mesons include pions and kaons.

Quark-Predictor. Murray Gell-Mann made sense of the subatomic zoo by proposing that protons, neutrons, and other subatomic particles that responded to the strong nuclear force were composed of smaller particles that he called quarks.

In that paper, Gell-Mann described three "flavors" of quarks, which he designated up, down, and strange (or u, d, and s). Protons are uud, while neutrons are ddu. Strange particles, of course, have strange quarks. He noted that quarks don't change flavor in strong interactions, but they do in weak interactions. That explained conservation of strangeness.

Beta decay is governed by the weak interaction. A down quark in a neutron transforms to an up quark, producing a proton. That process also produces an electron (the beta particle), and a neutrino. Thanks to Gell-Mann, the subatomic world was beginning to make more sense. The 1970s, however, brought about more surprises.

In 1974, two teams of physicists discovered another subatomic meson. One group wanted to call it J, and the other wanted to name it with the Greek letter psi. Physicists settled on using both, and so the J/psi particle went down in history. The discovery was considered historic because in 1964, Sheldon Glashow (1932–) and James Bjorken (1934–) had speculated about a fourth quark flavor they called charm (c). The J/psi fit their prediction of a meson composed of a charm and an anti-charm quark. The discovery of other charmed particles soon followed.

With that, the Standard Model of particle physics had begun to take shape. Normal atomic matter was made of two kinds of **leptons** (from the Greek word meaning small),

A Charming Result. Samuel Ting and his team display the discovery graph of a particle that came to be called J/psi. It was the first subatomic particle known to contain a charm quark.

electrons and neutrinos (now designated electron-neutrinos), and two flavors of quark (up and down). A more massive second generation of particles included two other leptons (muons and muon-neutrinos) plus strange and charm quarks.

Within a year of discovering the J/psi, physicists needed to reevaluate that model when they detected an even heavier version of the electron, which they designated by the Greek tau. Its behavior suggested that it had a partner neutrino. That immediately suggested the possibility of a third pair of quarks, which are now designated top (t) and bottom (b), though some physicists preferred to call them truth and beauty. By 1995, particle physicists had seen evidence of those as well.

By 2001, studies of neutrinos were indicating that the third generation of matter was the last to be expected. The Standard Model appeared to be complete with three generations of four particles (two leptons and two quarks). It also included other particles called **gauge bosons** that produced the fundamental forces when exchanged between the fundamental particles. For electromagnetism, the gauge bosons are photons. For strong interactions, the gauge bosons are called **gluons**. For the weak interaction, the gauge bosons were called W and Z.

All of those had been found, but one huge question remained unanswered: What gave those particles their different

What Is a Gauge Boson?

The subatomic zoo has several different categories with different names. For example, leptons, hadrons, mesons, and baryons have names referring to their size. The word **boson** comes from a different source. One of the quantum properties of a subatomic particle is called **spin**, and for bosons it takes values that are whole numbers times Planck's constant. (We use the term spin because quantum mechanics describes wave functions rather than particles in the traditional sense. Thus it is not accurate to speak of a particle as spinning on its axis.) Another set of particles called fermions, including protons, neurons, and electrons, have spins values that are odd numbers times half of Planck's constant.

Fermions obey Pauli's exclusion principal. Bosons do not. The mathematics of quantum mechanics includes statistical analysis of those two kinds of particles. The names come from pioneering physicists who developed the appropriate techniques. Fermions are named for Enrico Fermi, who named the neutrino among many other accomplishments. Bosons are named for Satyendra Nath Bose (1894–1974).

Gauge bosons are associated with the fundamental fields and forces. They give those forces or fields their scale, just as a gauge establishes the physical scale of many objects. Thus the Higgs boson is a gauge boson associated with the **Higgs field** that, as you will discover, gives particles their mass.

masses? The best explanation came from Peter Higgs, François Englert, and the others noted above. The search was on for the Higgs boson. Finding it or ruling it out would change the course of our understanding of the subatomic world.

4 THE HIGGS
Boson and Beyond

By the early 1960s, thanks to quantum mechanics, physicists viewed fundamental forces in a new way. Each one was the result of a field carried by subatomic particles called gauge bosons. The force associated with the field was the result of exchanging virtual gauge bosons. Electromagnetic forces resulted from the exchange of virtual photons. The strong force, which Yukawa initially described as the result of exchanging virtual pions, changed when physicists realized that quarks were the real fundamental particles, which exchanged gauge bosons called gluons as the glue that bound quarks together. And the weak force required bosons called the W and Z.

The forces are related to measureable properties of the particles, and the gauge bosons provide a scale to those interactions. The properties we measure in electromagnetism come from electric charge. The strong force comes from a property called **"color,"** which has nothing to do with light but is a convenient way to describe the way quarks combine to form mesons and baryons. The property that describes how particles relate to the weak interaction is sometimes called hypercharge. That is because the theory that led to the W and Z bosons also combined the weak force with electromagnetism. Physicists call the combined forces the electroweak interaction.

What about gravity? Since Einstein developed his general theory of relativity, physicists have considered gravity to be different from the other fundamental interactions. Instead of being a force, gravity is a property of space and time that causes masses to attract each other. Still, many theorists have proposed that gravitational attraction is the result of the exchange of gauge bosons called gravitons.

Whether or not gravitons exist, the developing Standard Model of particle physics needed a way to account for the difference in masses between the generations of leptons and quarks. In fact, they needed a way to account for mass itself. That is when Higgs, Englert, and the others entered the story with a new interaction.

Discovering and Measuring Subatomic Particles

That new interaction is now called the Higgs field. Like the other fields and forces, it is carried by a gauge boson called the Higgs boson. All known subatomic particles except photons and gluons respond to the Higgs field. Every other subatomic particle interacts with virtual Higgs bosons, and the strength of their interaction gives them mass.

The Higgs field explains the difference between electrons, muons, and taus. They are identical except that muons interact

THE STANDARD MODEL

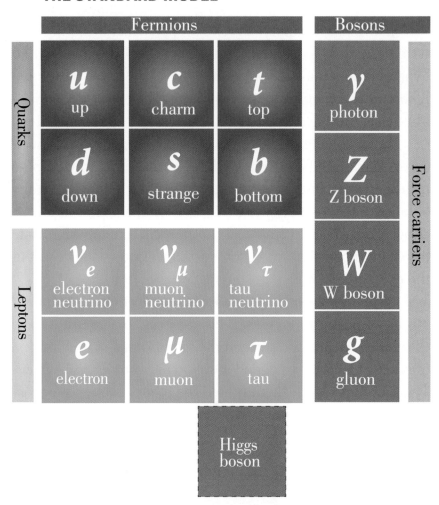

The Standard Model of Particle Physics. Each of the three left-hand columns of this diagram shows a generation of subatomic particles containing two quarks and two leptons. The mass of each generation increases from left to right. The rightmost column includes the gauge bosons of the electromagnetic, weak, and strong forces. The Higgs field and its boson are responsible for the different mass of each generation.

more strongly with the Higgs field than electrons, and taus interact with it more strongly than muons. Likewise the strangeness-charm pair of quarks interacts more strongly with the Higgs field than the up-down pair, giving them more mass. The top-bottom pair of quarks interact even more strongly, so they are the most massive quarks.

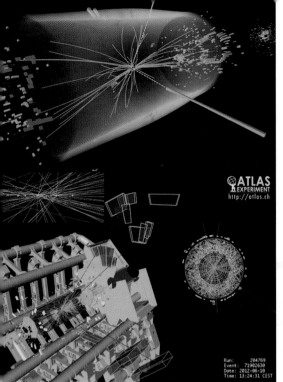

Breakthrough Discoveries. This diagram shows two of the events that confirmed the existence of the Higgs boson. The Higgs was detected indirectly by a "signature," or identifiable products of its decay. The top shows two muons resulting from a collision in the CMS detector. The lower event shows different perspectives of four photons produced by a collision in the ATLAS detector.

Still, as long as the Higgs boson and Higgs field remained undetected, they had to be considered hypothetical—educated guesses without evidence to support them. Because the Higgs seemed to be the last missing piece of the standard model, physicists made searching for it a high priority. But finding it would prove quite difficult.

The Standard Model predicted a range of masses that the Higgs might have. In order to find it, their particle accelerators needed to create enough energy in a collision to equal its mass, according to $E = mc^2$. Particle accelerators had advanced a long way since the early cyclotrons and linear accelerators. Still, to find the Higgs, they needed a new type of machine called a collider. Instead of merely accelerating a beam and smashing it into a target, colliders create two beams and send them toward each other.

Until CERN completed the Large Hadron Collider in 2008, the most powerful collider in the world was the Tevatron at the Fermi National Accelerator Laboratory outside of Chicago, Illinois. The Tevatron collided a beam of protons with a beam of antiprotons. Estimates of the Higgs boson's mass indicated that it might be detectable at the Tevatron's maximum energy. But even so, to be certain of what they found, the machine would have to run for a long period. The reason is that they would need very rare head-on collisions to create Higgs bosons, and even then, many different outcomes would result from those collisions.

Creating Higgs bosons would require millions of collisions, and detecting a Higgs would be rare even in those cases. The reason is that the Higgs does not have an electric charge, and uncharged particles do not leave a trail. The Higgs would have to be identified after it decays into charged particles, whose paths could be measured, or into detectable photons of light. Scientists refer to such events as the "signature" of the Higgs.

Inside the LHC. The Large Hadron Collider lies in a 17-mile- (27-kilometer-) long, underground, doughnut-shaped tunnel that crosses the border between Switzerland and France. Workers ride bicycles or small electric carts to inspect or repair the various parts of the collider, including its main beam pipes.

"The God Particle"

Some readers of this book may have heard the Higgs boson described as "The God Particle." That nickname comes from the title of a 1993 book about the Higgs boson written by Leon Lederman (1922–) and science writer Dick Teresi. For many years, Lederman was director of the Fermi National Accelerator Laboratory and won the 1988 Nobel Prize in physics for discovering the muon neutrino.

Lederman is considered an outstanding science communicator with a quirky and delightful sense of humor. Yet most physicists dislike the title of that book. In fact, the word "hate" might not be strong enough to describe their reaction to it. So it is not surprising that Lederman has been asked about it many times. He has given two different and quotable answers. The first is that the Higgs boson is "so crucial to our understanding of the structure of matter, yet so elusive, that I have given it a nickname." The second is that the publisher wouldn't let him call it "The [gosh darn] Particle, though that might be a more appropriate title, given its villainous nature and all the trouble it is causing."

Since the publisher has the final say about a book's title, the second explanation may be closer to the truth.

Lederman Displays His Sense of Humor. Particle physicist Leon Lederman was a long-time director of the Fermi National Accelerator Laboratory, home of the Tevatron. Second only to his scientific accomplishments, he is noted for a delightful sense of humor, on display here with his "mini-me" and in the subtitle of his book about the Higgs boson, *The God Particle: If the Universe Is the Answer, What Is the Question?*

Even detecting the signature is not enough. Particle physicists need to rule out other collisions or decays that could possibly produce that same or a very similar pattern in the detectors. That required detecting enough data to statistically rule out all other possibilities to an extremely high level of confidence. That is why they needed a machine that not only produced higher energies in collisions, but also had more intense beams so that they could gather enough data. That machine was the LHC.

The illustration on page 49 shows two events where the Higgs boson produced a particular signature. The top event, produced by the CMS detector, shows a pair of muons emitted together. The lower event, which comes from the ATLAS detector team, shows four photons emerging from the collision. They are very brief snapshots and show many of the complications the physicists faced. Note all the tracks from other decays and collisions in the detector. It took a lot of computer power to analyze millions of candidate events studied over several months of running the LHC to confirm what they had found. Its mass turned out to be more than 130 times as heavy as a proton.

The Final Word?

The discovery of the Higgs boson at the LHC may close one book on the Standard Model of Particle Physics, but it is unlikely to be the final word. Some versions of the Higgs theory have not one but several bosons. Those other bosons are expected to be more massive than the particles that the Large Hadron Collider has been able to generate so far. But because of a design flaw, the LHC has been operating at lower power levels and beam intensities than its original engineering goal.

The Final Weld. A worker makes the final weld on the Superconducting Magnets and Circuits Consolidation (SMACC) project on May 28, 2014. SMACC is a major part of the repairs and upgrades during the two-year planned shutdown of the LHC after its successful search for the Higgs boson.

To reach maximum energy and capacity, engineers shut down the machine and began a series of upgrades and repairs during 2013 and 2014. After its restart in 2015, it has begun to gradually increase its energy and beam strength. That will allow it to explore the subatomic world for other more massive particles. No one knows what to expect, but nature is always full of surprises.

In coming years, the LHC will not only be exploring the subatomic world, but also the universe as a whole. It may or may not find more massive Higgs bosons or other unpredicted particles. But it will definitely reveal what the very early universe was like immediately after "the Big Bang" that led to the cosmos we know today. Cosmologists can only make educated guesses about what happens when matter is concentrated in the hot dense state that existed at the universe's beginning. Thanks to the most energetic collisions in the LHC, they will be able to make measurements under conditions like those earliest instants of time.

Glossary

alpha particle (or **alpha ray**) A helium nucleus that is
emitted from some radioactive elements.

atom The smallest bit of matter than can be identified as a
certain chemical element.

atomic mass or **atomic weight** A number that specifies the
mass of the atoms of a particular element. For naturally
occurring elements, it is approximately equal to the
number of protons plus the average number of neutrons
in the nuclei.

atomic number The number of protons in the nucleus of
an atom, which determines its chemical identity as
an element.

beta particle or **beta ray** An electron that is emitted from
some radioactive elements.

boson A subatomic particle whose spin quantum number is
a whole number times Planck's constant.

Brownian motion The jiggling motion of a piece of dust or
pollen suspended in a fluid; first observed by Robert
Brown and eventually shown by Albert Einstein to
demonstrate the existence of atoms and molecules.

color In the theory of the strong nuclear force, this term is used to refer to the property that particles have that makes them respond to the force, just as electric charge is a property of particles that makes them respond to electromagnetic forces. It has no connection with the visual color of an object or of light.

compound A substance made of only one kind of molecule that consists of more than one kind of atom.

electromagnetism A fundamental force of nature, or property of matter and energy (such as light), that includes electricity, magnetism, and electromagnetic waves.

gamma ray A high-energy photon that is emitted from some radioactive elements.

gauge boson A type of boson associated with a fundamental field or force. It gives that force or field a scale to establish its strength, just as a gauge establishes the physical scale of many objects.

gluon A particle that is exchanged between quarks, resulting in their being bound together.

Higgs field and **Higgs boson** The Higgs field is a fundamental property of space that interacts with most subatomic particles to give them mass through the exchange of virtual gauge bosons. The field and bosons are named after Peter Higgs, the first person to propose a theory that included both.

lepton A subatomic particle that does not respond to the strong nuclear force. The leptons include electrons, muons, taus, and their corresponding neutrinos.

molecule The smallest bit of matter that can be identified as a certain chemical compound.

nucleus (plural nuclei) The very tiny, positively charged central part of an atom that carries most of the atom's mass.

periodic table of the elements An arrangement of the elements in rows and columns by increasing atomic number, first proposed by Dmitri Mendeleyev, in which elements in the same column have similar chemical properties.

photoelectric effect A phenomenon in which light can, under some circumstances, knock electrons out of atoms. Einstein's explanation of this effect led to scientific acceptance of the photon as a particle and eventually to quantum mechanics.

quantum (plural quanta) A tiny basic particle of matter or packet of energy, first discovered in light but then found to apply to matter as well.

quantum mechanics A field of physics developed to describe the relationships between matter and energy that accounts for the dual wave-particle nature of both.

quantum number One of several numbers that specifies the state of a property of a subatomic particle, such as its orbital characteristics within an atom or its spin.

quark A sub-subatomic particle that exists in several forms that combine to make protons, neutrons, and some other subatomic particles.

radioactivity A property of unstable atoms that causes them to emit alpha, beta, or gamma rays.

scattering An experimental technique used to detect the shape or properties of an unseen object by observing how other objects deflect from it.

spectrum (plural spectra) The mixture of colors contained within a beam of light, or the band produced when those colors are spread out by a prism or other device that separates the colors from each other.

spin A quantum number describing a property of a subatomic particle as if it were spinning on an axis. Quantum mechanics deals with wave functions rather than particles, so it is inaccurate to speak of a particle that actually has an axis and spins. Rather, it describes the particle as having a property called spin.

strong nuclear force, strong interaction, or **strong force** A fundamental force of nature that acts to hold the protons and neutrons in a nucleus together.

theory of relativity A theory developed by Albert Einstein that dealt with the relationship between space and time. Its most famous equation ($E = mc^2$) described the relationship between mass and energy.

weak nuclear force, weak interaction, or **weak force** A fundamental force of nature that is responsible for the beta decay of a radioactive nucleus.

For Further
Information

Books

Bortz, Fred. *Seven Wonders of Exploration Technology.* Minneapolis, MN: Twenty-First Century Books, 2010.

Bortz, Fred. *The Periodic Table of Elements and Dmitry Mendeleyev.* New York: Rosen, 2014.

Bortz, Fred. *Physics: Decade by Decade.* Twentieth-Century Science. New York: Facts On File, 2007.

Fernandes, Bonnie Juettner. *The Large Hadron Collider.* Chicago: Norwood House Press, 2014.

Green, Dan, and Simon Basher. *Extreme Physics.* New York: Kingfisher, 2013.

Hagler, Gina. *Discovering Quantum Mechanics.* New York: Rosen, 2015.

Marsico, Katie. *Key Discoveries in Physical Science.* Minneapolis, MN: Lerner Publications, 2015.

Morgan, Sally. *From Greek Atoms to Quarks: Discovering Atoms.* New York: Heinemann Publishing, 2008.

Websites

American Institute of Physics Center for the History of Physics
www.aip.org/history-programs/physics-history

This site includes several valuable online exhibits on the history of physics, including The Discovery of the Electron (www.aip.org/history/electron/jjhome.htm).

European Organization for Nuclear Research (CERN)
home.web.cern.ch/students-educators

CERN has an extensive online educational site, including information about the Large Hadron Collider and the Higgs boson.

The Nobel Foundation Prizes for Physics
www.nobelprize.org/nobel_prizes/physics

Learn more about every Nobel Prize since 1901. This site includes biographies, Nobel Lectures, interviews, photos, articles, video clips, educational games, and much more.

Museums and Institutes

American Institute of Physics
Center for the History of Physics
One Physics Ellipse
College Park, MD 20740
(301) 209-3165
www.aip.org/history-programs/physics-history

The Center for the History of Physics houses a research library and a photo archive, and has created numerous online resources in all areas of physics.

Dmitry Mendeleyev Museum and Archive of Saint Petersburg State University
Universitetskaya naberezhnaya, d. 7/9
St. Petersburg 199034
Russia
(812) 328-97-44

According to the website chemheritage.org, in a review of the museum (www.chemheritage.org/discover/media/magazine/articles/26-2-mendeleev-at-home.aspx), the collection includes artifacts from Mendeleyev's life and work.

Ernest Rutherford Collection
Room 111 Ernest Rutherford Physics Building
McGill University
3600 rue University
Montréal, QC H3A 2T8
Canada
(514) 398-6490
www.mcgill.ca/historicalcollections/departmental/ernest-rutherford

The Rutherford Museum contains the apparatus used by Nobel Prize winner Ernest Rutherford when he was Professor of Experimental Physics at McGill from 1898 to 1907. The collection includes letters, documents, memorabilia, photographs of Rutherford and his colleagues, and other materials relating to Rutherford's work, including the desk he used in his home.

Lederman Science Education Center

Fermilab MS 777
Box 500
Batavia, IL 60510
(630) 840-8258
ed.fnal.gov/lsc/lscvideo/index.shtml

This museum is an outstanding place to discover the science and history of subatomic particles. It is located at the Fermi National Accelerator Laboratory (Fermilab) outside of Chicago.

Ontario Science Centre

770 Don Mills Road
Toronto, ON M3C 1T3
Canada
(416) 696-1000
www.ontariosciencecentre.ca

The Ontario Science Centre is Canada's leading science and technology museum. Its programs and exhibits aim to inspire a lifelong journey of curiosity, discovery, and action to create a better future for the planet.

Index

Page numbers in **boldface** are illustrations. Entries in **boldface** are glossary terms.

About the Author

Award-winning children's author **Fred Bortz** spent the first twenty-five years of his working career as a physicist, gaining experience in fields as varied as nuclear reactor design, automobile engine control systems, and science education. He earned his PhD at Carnegie Mellon University, where he also worked in several research groups from 1979 through 1994. He has been a full-time writer since 1996.